RIVER
OF TRUTH

A Poetic Experience

ISAAC BROWN JR

"River Of Truth" A Poetic Experience

Copyright © 2025 Isaac Brown Jr
ISBN: 978-1-7363362-2-9 paperback

Library of Congress Control Number: 2025911632

No part of this publication may be reproduced, distributed, stored in a retrieval system, or transmitted in any form or by any means, including photocopying, recording, or other electronic or mechanical methods, without the prior written permission of the publisher, except for brief quotations in critical reviews, articles, or certain noncommercial uses permitted by copyright law. For permission requests, write to the publisher at: ikeseesyou@gmail.com.

Author images displayed on the front and back book covers and the introduction page, were photographed by my wonderful wife, Cynthia Lynn Brown. All other images were taken by the author, Isaac Brown Jr. All river scene pictures (Delaware River) were photographed at Battery Park, located in New Castle, Delaware.

Note: The author's staff was crafted by the late great Lester L. Harris of Oxford, Pennsylvania.

Ordering Information
Books may be purchased in large quantities at a discount for educational, business, or sales promotional use. For information, email ikeseesyou@gmail.com.

Published by Isaac Brown Jr, 4 Streams Series, LLC
City of Publication: New Castle, Delaware
Project Management: Spoonfed Motivation Publications

FOREWORD

> Nina Simone said, "It is an artist's duty to reflect the time in which we live."

River of Truth is a poetic reflection of the current but familiar struggle of humanity. Like the ebbs and flows of a river we find ourselves flowing into a realm of poetic wonder. The pages that follow are not merely ink and paper but a wave of emotions colliding with the shores of human experience and imagination.

Each poetic story within this collection is an invitation to embark on a journey of introspection and discovery. As you travel the river, the tide will feel familiar yet strange. As you reflect on your own truth, whether love, loss, or the eternal quest for meaning, the desire is that these poetic stories will resonate deep within your soul.

As you turn each page, allow the lyrical prose and the rhythm of the sentences carry you like the gentle lull of waves upon the shore. Allow the stories to envelop you, to transport you to places unseen and feelings not yet realized. In this book, you will be challenged to look within; to remember the power of love and its ability to be a "bridge over troubled waters."

Welcome to a world where words are not just read but felt, where stories are not just told but lived. May these poetic short stories leave an indelible mark upon your heart and kindle the flame of wonder within your soul. May the river lead you to the freedom that the love of God provides, when we return to His truth.

Cynthia Lynn Brown, BSN, RN, FCN

ACKNOWLEDGMENTS

Special thanks to my best-of-the-best wife, Cynthia Lynn Brown. Thank you for your felt and demonstrated support. Your excellently written forward and several readings and critiques of my **River of Truth** book project were invaluable to me. Also, I highly appreciate your words of encouragement and your evening treks along the Delaware River to take pictures for my book. You were always there for me and never complained. For me, you are the best wife in the known and unknown universe! God bless you always!!!

Love you always, your forever devoted husband,
Ike Brown Jr

A big thank you to all who purchased and read my previous book, **I See You.** Additionally, I appreciate all those who attended the various open mics to see me perform my poetry. Also, family and friends, thank you for attentively listening to me recite my poetry at backyard outings and other events! And to my great publishing consultant-coach, Dr. Cherita Weatherspoon (Spoonfed Motivation Publications) thank you for your demonstrated expertise and unblemished integrity! May every one of you receive God's endless blessings!

INTRODUCTION

You have had or do have an opportunity to join me with the I-See-You-Poetic Experience, as written in my first book, **I See You**. But now, please join me and travel down the **River of Truth**. A poetically written book based on my life experiences, observations, and insights.

It is not my goal to convince you to believe everything that I write. What I write is my interpretation of truth; and you have yours. My goal is for you to read, think about, and discuss the things I write with someone else. Subsequently, maybe some of you will be motivated to make this world a little better. In continuance, my hope and prayer is that we increase our love for God, humanity, and ourselves as we travel down THE **River of Truth**!

Happy travels, Isaac Brown Jr

TABLE OF CONTENTS

I. River of Truth 1
  1. "Follow the Son" 3
  2. "You Are My Story" 8
  3. "I Am That I Am" 10
  4. "The Question" 12
  5. "What If" 14
  6. "River Of Truth" 16

II. Race To Be Seen 19
  1. "All I Want Is Justice" 21
  2. "Mom" 23
  3. "Fire In The ICE" 26
  4. "The Picture" 29
  5. "Say You See Me Too" 33
  6. "Other Man And Brother Man" 37
  7. "You Do Not See" 40
  8. "When The Blind Lead Those That See" 42

III. A Piece of Peace 45
   1. "I Am An American". 47
   2. "I Pledge Allegiance". 50
   3. "Judas Goats". 52
   4. "Hurt Kills" 56
   5. "Men at War" 58
   6. "Civil War". 63
   7. "Weapons of Instruction" 65

IV. Truth or Consequences. 69
   1. "It Is What It Is" 71
   2. "When the Skies Were Blue". 74
   3. "Beautiful Sunsets". 76
   4. "In The State of California". 78
   5. "Slave Meals". 80
   6. "Dead and Gone" 84

V. Swimming Upstream 87
   1. "Just A Thought". 89
   2. "Me Version of The King's English" 90
   3. "Mothers Man-boys and Deadbeat Dads". 93
   4. "Users Are Losers". 96
   5. "Holler Happy Holidays" 99
   6. "A Stain In the Rain". 102

VI. Speak Love 107

   1. "Speak Love" (prologue) 109

   2. "Looking for A Good Knight" 111

   3. "Boys And Men, A Lover's Anthem" 115

   4. "She Is A Woman (A Message To Our Men)" 118

   5. "Love Yourself" 119

   6. "Long-stem Roses" 121

   7. "Speak Love" (epilogue) 124

VII. The River Speaks 127

   1. "I Still See You" 129

   2. "Men of God" 131

   3. "Denominations the Religion Division" 137

   4. "Stop In the Name of God" 140

   5. "Sin No More" 143

   6. "Return to Thee" 146

   7. "I Call Your Name" 150

About the Author 155

CHAPTER 1

RIVER OF TRUTH

"Follow the Son"

As I gazed upon a great river
The river found my eyes
And a bright light appeared
Under the distant horizon

The light drew me towards it
And beckoned me to swim
Upstream
Against the current

It seemed to pull my very soul

I was afraid
For last night's full moon
And today's winding winds
Created a sense of chaos

The waves constantly clashed
With so much ferocity
That they seemed to foam
With an animated anger

But the light had a serenity
That seemed to pull me
Away from my mounting fear

River of Truth

I gathered all my strength
And entered the river

I swam with all my might
Towards the light
Which gave me strength

Then I looked back and saw
Many people effortlessly
Swimming with the current

They traveled towards a huge ship
The ships surface had iridescent lights
But the cabins below
Were ominously dark

Loud music seemed to play
In many languages
That I could not discern

I felt the ship and the raging current
Pulling me to turn around
I began to question my decision
To swim towards the light

But as I looked at the smiling faces
That passed by me
Their expressions became empty
And seemed to be
Void of thought and substance

I was afraid to look directly
Into their eyes
For their eyes dilated
With the flashing lights of the ship

So I began to swim harder
Upstream
Towards the light

But fear and doubt continued
To haunt my mind from the memory
Of the many people I passed

The gravity of those thoughts
Tempted me to reverse my course
And swim towards
The great big beautiful ship

I struggled to continue my swim
Against the strong current

Just when I felt I had
Nothing else to give
I began to weaken
And almost passed out

The current swept me into a crevice
Of a large weathered tree limb
It was the limb of an old crusted tree
That seemed to bend towards the light

River of Truth

Even with the loss
Of such an arm-like limb
It had stood stately
By the edge of the river's shore

But the light called me
It knew my name
It shined so bright
That it renewed my energy

I let go of the tree limb
And swam
With a sense of purpose

Sometimes I hit rocks
But I continued to swim

Other times I passed whirlpools
That tried to suck me
Into their enticing dance

But I continued to swim

Many people passed by me
From the opposite direction

I recognized them
And they encouraged me
To turn around and join them

But I continued to swim

As I got closer to the light
I began to feel its omnipresence

Peace and restoration
Suddenly hit me

As I reached the pinnacle of my journey
The water became calm

I was ecstatic at the magnificence
Of the manifested glory of the light

For the light had taken form
And became
The Beautiful Son
And
The River of Truth

"You Are My Story"

Friends and family
It was you
With God's blessings
That made me strong

Strong enough to resist
All kinds of evil

For you modeled for me
Something better to belong
A part of God's tapestry
Written in the heavens

You were and are my story

You fed me
With words of love
And reassurance

Giving me just what I needed
To be a strong man of integrity
And patient endurance

I am what I am because
You are who you are
And

Each of you
Made me
What I am in your heart

You are my story

Through your example
You taught me
That my greatest wealth
Was to believe in God
Family friends and myself

So l thank God
In all his glory
For choosing each of you
To help me write
My story

"I Am That I Am"

What you call me
Retarded stupid slow underdeveloped
Does not matter

If you call me
Runt giant skinny fat or extra wide
It does not matter
And I will not hide

I may be the whitest white the darkest black
The reddest red the yellowest yellow
Or the odd man out albino fellow

Still
It does not matter

Call me outsider different inferior and sad
Even if you profile me guilty of everything bad
It does not matter

Because in your ignorance pride and insecurity
You project all the ugly you are unto me
And you are far more screwed up
Than what you think you see

But it does not matter
Because I am that I am

Consequently
Only God can change or define me
And He has already defined me as

I am that I am
A Perfect Me

"The Question"

What is the question
You should be asking
When the answer
Is hidden by all you believe

How can you find
What is not really lost
When you open your eyes and see
Only what you want to see

Do you not ask the question
Whose answer you already know
But are too afraid to speak
Into the atmosphere

Are you fearful that the truth
Will expose you so profoundly
That what you believe
Will have to disappear

And all your lies will be
Manifested in such a way
That the powerful person
You think you are will fade away

You answer the questions
That define who you think you are

But are you too afraid
To answer the question
That reminds you
Of who you are not

"What If"

What if we did not make pretend to love everyone
But really loved everyone
What if you loved me unconditionally and
What if I loved you more than you loved me

What if we said hello not with our mouth
But with our heart
What if we treated everyone
Like they are a bright shining star

What if we looked at differences
Of race color and ethnicities
As a way to make a better you
And a better me

What if we treated our body
Like our desire to live longer
What if we stopped wasting our food
And shared it to end world hunger

What if we treated our environment
Like we loved our dependents
And our descendants

What if we poured into others
What we want to come back to ourselves

What if we treated
And respected our children
Like we want the world
To treat and respect them

What if we changed the atmosphere
With a love so strong and full of trust
That others would feel the full power
Of The Son through us

What if we professed
To walk in the spirit
And not in the flesh

What if we could convince each other
That no one is better than anyone else

But together
We
Make a better person

What if

"River Of Truth"

Let humankind find a shared love
A love that flows

Like a river of truth that delivers

The kind of love-filled energy
That sets even our ancestors free

Free to stand on the riverbanks
And give thanks to the Almighty

Let love flow like a river of truth
So powerful
That the entire human race
Will resonate in a way
That all can hear it

A unifying spirit running through
The deep forest of despair
Destroying fear and hatred
Everywhere

As many diverse streams
Come together
They will rise over the mountain top
To see Martin Luther King Junior's dream

Where all God's children
Must stop
And bow and unite
To the Ultimate Sacrifice

As they flow like a river moved
By the Truth the Way and the Life
Jesus The Christ
Flowing with brightness

He is The Son
Forming out of many
Only One

One face
The human race

And everyone
Looks like me and you
Flowing flowing flowing

Flowing like a river
Of love and truth

CHAPTER II

RACE TO BE SEEN

"All I Want Is Justice"

How could it be
What you say it is
When it is not
What you say

A half-truth is
A whole lie
Today
And every day

All I want is justice
Justice justice
All I want is justice
Justice justice

It does not matter
What you say
I will not ever walk away
I am making my stand today

All I want is justice
Justice justice
All I want is justice
Justice justice

Do you see
My tears falling
Can't you hear
My heart calling

All I want is justice
Justice justice
All
 I
Want

Is justice
Justice justice

"Mom"

Mom
I hear the screams of black men
Kicked to the ground
Dreams being beat away
Punched away sprayed away

As their screams turn
Into inaudible sounds

It is where the inhumanity of
The invisible of humanity
Is lost
And never found

Mom
Let them know I to feel pain
And sometimes I cry

But please tell them
I want to live
 I want to live
I do not want to die

Let them see I am a man too
Though I struggle sometimes
Just like others do

River of Truth

Mom
I am your son
Why can't they see
What you see

A breathing human being
Who loves and is loved on this earth
A husband father uncle friend
I smile I laugh and sometimes I hurt

Mom
I have so much more to give
You know I am not an animal
I am not a beast

Maybe they could see clearer
If they took off their sheets

Mom
Why do they get so mad
No matter what they say
It hurts so bad
When they treat me this way

Mom
I am crying
As I hear them laughing
And lying

But the truth
Will have its day

Mom
Why don't they see me
Why can't they believe me
Why don't they leave me alone

I just want to come home

Mom
Do not be bereaved
Just forgive them for they
Know not what they do

Momma momma
I cannot breathe
Looks like I will see heaven
Before I see you

I love you Mom

"Fire In The ICE"

There is fire fire
Fire in the ICE
Separating families
Even those that are nice

Kicking in strange doors
Just like they are at war
There is fire fire
Fire in the ICE

Oh for heaven's sake
Are we a police state
Displacing needy people
From the land of the free
Afraid of colorizing America
With minorities

So now they are displaced
Mainly because of race
There is fire fire
Fire in the ICE

Distorting the law
And the constitution
Hurting one hurts all
With this prejudiced solution

Except for stolen lands
From the Mexicans
African slavery
And Indian eliminations

We are a nation
Formed from immigration
But those were mostly European
So now they hate what they are seeing

There is fire fire
Fire in the ICE

Trumping what is right
Autocrats and plutocrats
Steer this racist ship
Trying their best to create
Their own dictatorship

Using their gestapo
Masqueraded as police
They terrorize families
And steal all their peace

As they overextend their powers
They rob us of ours
But all people will pay the price

Because there is fire fire
Fire in the ICE
Fire fire fire in the ICE

There is fire fire
Fire in the ICE
Fire fire fire in the ICE

Fire ICE!

"The Picture"

This is not a tall tail
This story is unfortunately true
I spent some time in jail
Accused of things I did not do

And to add to the curse
The cops never read me
The Miranda verse

As they surrounded me
I was emotionally tested
Because I did not know why
I was stopped and suddenly arrested

I was put in jail for murder
And several other alleged crimes
They had the real criminal's mug shot
Which looked nothing like mine

But their racist eyes
Were diversity blind
For he had a face so fat that
Just like I said before
It looked nothing like mine

I wondered what did they see
The criminal in their picture
Was three shades lighter than me

River of Truth

I should have been released
As soon as they saw the picture
But I was a poor man's son
Who would have not been arrested
If my parents were a lot richer

Or maybe if I were white
I would have received
Much more than my
Neglected legal rights

But I did not cuss
Or even put up a fight
Even though I suspected
Those policemen thought

We all look alike

A splatter of a portrait
Taken for granted
Another black man in jail
Another life transplanted

I was treated like an
Unanimated fixture

But I was being profiled
Handcuffed
Jailed
And forced to have

My picture
Snapped without a smile

Though the police
Had to know I was innocent
Just based on comparing
The real criminal's picture
With my profile

So I became a dark figure
Standing against the jail cell wall
In a barred room much too small
And no one who cared about me
Knew about the uninvited police call

I committed to go on a fast
Until they would let me out

Then at last a black cop
Looked at the criminal's picture
And started to shout
From deep within

You know... well
This poor guy
Looks nothing like him

It took me years
To talk about this
But the memories
Are still green

River of Truth

I wish they were just
My imagination
Or a made-up story
For the movie screen

A joke
Or a big boy bluff
With boys in blue
Trying to act tuff

But to be real
I was almost crying
From the tightness
Of my handcuffs

Though I believe most police
Are good women and men
I think about the innocently incarcerated
Whose stories had a much worse end

Sometimes my eyes get wet
As I hold back tears
And the thoughts
That are hard to forget

All that unwelcomed drama
Can give one PSBT
Police Stressed Blackman's Trauma
Caused by being profiled
For just being me

"Say You See Me Too"

Do you see me
Like I see you
Then say you see me too

Do you judge me for who I am
Or by falsified statistics
Do you just see my darkness
Or my characteristics

Do you notice the royalty
Radiating from my dark skin
Or the other nuances accrued
Then say you see me too

Do not just say hello and good-bye
Without looking into my eyes
Or shake my hand
Like a weak man wanting to cry

Do not just see my race
Without noticing
The contours of my face

Do you see that I have narrow eyes
A nose that is medium-thick
And lips that are average size

River of Truth

All these things you would realize
As true
If you were seeing me
As a human being just like you

Do not swerve on the sidewalk
When I pass by you
Then have the nerve to say
Hi or how do you do

But hoping my answer
Does not involve
Spending time with you

When you see
My dark face
Do I reflect something
You want to erase

Or someone
You would like to
Invite
Over to your place

Or is that not your way
Because you are afraid of
What others might say

When I look at you
I see all of you

So please
Say you see me too

Do we all look alike
Because you do not
Take the time to
Really look at me

Like a forest
With many trees
Some point to the east
Others point to the west

Some are small
Some are tall
But all are different
Then all the rest

People are the same
And if you really looked at me
You would see past my names

Brown Pulaski Di Sabatino
Wang Li and Abdul

And with no interference
About my appearance
You would say
You see me too

River of Truth

I am orange red black white
Yellow brown and shades in between
But your prejudice
Makes me hard to be seen

Do not be in a hurry
Or be fearful of the view
You do not have to worry
For I acknowledge you

So look me
In my eyes
And say
You see me too

"Other Man And Brother Man"

To understand American
You have got to understand
Other man and brother man

I am a brother man
And
Justice don't trust us
It just bust us
For looking like dark dust

Standing on the corner
Looking like
A fabricated crime

The brother man
Gets viewed
As a negative news celebrity
Most of the time

But other man
Is so sanctified
That when he commits a crime
He rarely gets identified

And when he does
They say he just had
A mental breakdown
But brother man gets

River of Truth

An identity shakedown

He gets identified as an
Animal a beast or clown
Getting lost in the system
And never found

He gets the unwanted favor
Of giving free labor
Hidden in prisons
That test his behavior

Other man
Just gets a slap on his hand
As his picture gets a waiver
From the newspaper stand

While the brother man's
Character gets swiped
In negative stereotypes

Other man gets cast
As people we like
A mother father daughter son
So they are forgiven
For the cruelty they have done

Other man gets a chance
Even when they have a gun

They get
Positive coverage on TV

While brother man
Gets cast
As the evil one

Brotherman gets a lifetime sentence
Of stress
Produced by prejudice
Just for being a minority

Please do not believe the hype
Of all those negative stereotypes
Because other man and brother man
Are less different than they are unalike

Like my mother used to say
There are two kinds of people
Good and bad
They come in all colors
Races and other forms of diversity

But it is so sad
That we separate based on that
Which we do not understand

Causing us to see
Another kind of separation
Brother man and other man

"You Do Not See"

You do not see what we see
Because you are who you are
And what we see is a
Different reality

We have a black perspective
That must be reflected
And protected
Otherwise it gets disrespected

So some of us cried
When you eliminated DEI
For we have lived long enough
To understand the reasons
Behind the whys

And when we look at your news
We see the blues
A eurocentric picture
With all the white fixtures

That does not show the truth
Of how we live
How we think
And why we do what we do

It is an alternate reality
That looks like fantasy

To people like me
Because you do not see
What we see

When you see the stars and stripes
And sing songs of praise
We see the stripes of our ancestors
That sent them to their graves

The statues of your leaders
Standing tall and made of rock
Are nothing but symbols to us
Of wealthy men who bought
Our ancestors off slavery blocks

You worship them as your heroes
And celebrate their bravery
But many of your heroes
Forced our ancestors into slavery

You do not feel our pain
Or know our perspective
But I am willing to explain
If you are willing
To listen and be respective

"When The Blind Lead Those That See"

Sometimes the blind
Will lead those that see
When those that see
Willingly
Follow blindly

It seems to happen when
Those with sight
And ability

Become too weak
To do what is right
And lead with responsibility

They will know what to do
But they will act like
They are doing something
Entirely brand new

And like a baby
They will allow
The blind and weak

To lead them around
Like their mind has
A diaper leak

Then they will use
The media and news
To drop their mental feces
All over you and I

In full public view
They will allow the blind
To fully bully them
Into doing
Just what they want them to do

They will not question
The things they see
Then expect the rest of us
To follow them blindly

They know
Some of us will follow them
Regardless of what is seen

Because their will is weak
Some will seek
To believe a lie
That promises them

All that they want
Rather than
What they truly need
To survive

River of Truth

The blind have a power
Stronger than those with sight
The ability to repeat lies
Until what is wrong seems right

Those that see will act like
They do not have a mind
And cults will be formed
Taught by the blind

As they lose self-control

Those with sight
Will give the blind
Additional rights
To distort what they
Once believed to be reality

This tragedy will cause
All to live in darkness
When the blind lead
Those that see

CHAPTER III

A PIECE OF PEACE

"I Am An American"

Many people I have saved
Many people I have put in graves
I have welcomed the oppressed
As I have oppressed some of the best

I am a dichotomy

Made up of those people
The ones I call the others
And those like me
The ones I call
Sisters and brothers

I am an American

My laws provide refuge
For the suffering
As my extravagance
Requires them to suffer

I show tremendous compassion
To those who melt into my pot
But not with those whose reaction
Is to protest about
The haves and the have-nots

River of Truth

I believe in capitalism
When the laws are written in my favor
But have no problem creating
Premeditated schisms
For those who oppose my behavior

I am a patriot

But have a violent reaction
With those who challenge
How the privileged and wealthy
Got what they got

I despise those who protest our flag
Do not they know how to act
When they kneel on their knees
While I am standing on their back

I am an American

I like to white my own story
And erase others' misery
But the others want to destroy us
By telling their WOKE history

I am an American

My blood runs pure
So do not come here
If you are from the wrong shores

I am an American

Sweet land of liberty
To those who agree with
The majority
And those who look like
And act like me

"I Pledge Allegiance"

I pledge allegiance
To flag the truth
From the
Disunited States of America

Because what I hear
Does not match what people do
Though since our childhood

We are brainwashed
With monomania
To robotically pledge allegiance
To words that are not true

Said words created by
A privileged public
For which it stands
Under a violent obedience
To be a gun nation under God

Where much was taken
From indigenous nations
And intentionally
Marginalized people
Were enslaved

Controlled
And robbed
By those whose wealth
Became indivisible

Through the creation of laws
That disproportionally
Served their selves
And their servant
Miseducated mobs

I do pledge allegiance
To our nation
But not to words
That hide discrimination
And liberty
And justice for all

Is on perpetual recall

"Judas Goats"

(A Judas Goat will lead sheep to slaughter while its own life is spared)

Environmental disaster
Cannot get there any faster
Don't need planes cars or boats
Just following government
Judas goats

A bunch of environmental deniers
And pied piper carbon hypers
That is what they do
With Co2

They do not care
When they pollute the air

They just want you to follow
The manufactured leaders
And other maligned media feeders

As they travel through your mind
They brainwash you with movies
Soap operas and reality shows
And other made-up skits

So that you do not know
You are acting
According to their script

Got you dependent on
Gasoline and oil
As they spray poison into
The earth's soil

Spending more money on
Their space program
They destroy the earth
And leave us with
Contaminated air and dirt

They build their
Bomb proof bunkers
Then try to please us
By shouting hallelujah Jesus

It ain't nothing but a scam
That takes our taxes
So they can escape to space
To rape other planetary lands

They got us brainwashed
To follow them
Where they are not going
Knowing
That is what we will do

River of Truth

Judas goats got us spending
Big-time money for fancy labels
With some not taking care of
Their children and bills
Even when they are able

Got us addicted to the thrill
Of acting like we are stable

We lose our minds and money
Pacifying ourselves
By eating bad food
That makes our stomach bloat

But we never waiver
We just beg favor
From the Judas goats

Then we go outside
To sit in the sun
And dream about how we
Can buy some fun

But we are controlled
By their hypnotic advertisements

Which are nothing but baptizements
Of intellectual disenfranchisements

With open eyes we sleep
And it ain't no joke
As our ancestors weep
When we follow the dreams
Created by the elites

And their army
Of Judas goats

"Hurt Kills"

Slow death
Prolonged pain
All spent
Nothing gained

Cannot forgive
Cannot live
No peace
No thrill
Feeling weak

Hurt kills

Boomerang
Dirt comes back
Sorry is late
Cannot escape
Heart attack
Made of hate

Made you brake
Take some pills
Everyday

Hurt kills

Your pain
Cannot keep

You destroy
Others weep
Time is lost
Cannot complete

You project
All you are
Reject the hate
Heal the scars

Hurt Kills

People scorned
Loved ones gone
You regret
But lose a turn
You abuse
Then you burn

Heal yourself
So you can love
Child inside
Can grow up

Think you are tough
Not enough
Because the hurt you feel
Is the hurt that kills

"Men at War"

It is not by chance or happenstance
That women give birth to men
Only to lose them
Time after time again
To the evolution of boys to men

They start out as boys
Who play with violent games
That use graphic video
Embedded in consoles
That cannot console a soul

Without buffering
They seem to rejoice
While playing their new games
That fail to show suffering
In their violent games of choice

There is no more hitting with sticks
There is only trick or trick
And that is not fun
When they shoot with loaded guns

Still they rejoice playing
King of the hill
Because the thrill seems to overcome
The sins of the kill

They soon develop
An insensitivity to all of humanity
As they divide into warring groups
With unreconciled insanity

They attempt to hide their barbarism
Through rules of engagement
And international laws
Of controlled violence
That all are willing to violate
Even if all shall fall

They placate their conscience
As they condone collateral damage
And the false notion
That the end
Justifies being mean

As we the people
Try to understand
Why civilized nations
Will not share resources and land

Or why man chooses to destroy
Civilizations in the name of
Preserving civilizations

So they keep us guessing
Trying to figure out
How civilized men

Can kill each other
As they dress up in
Religious garb
And recite immoral garbage

Trying to seek God's blessings
They beg to have the right to
Destroy each other again and again
All without admitting their own sin

They do not know
Or simply forget to understand
What it truly means
To be a true man of God

But time and time again
They make the ungodly decision
To kill others
In the name of religion

Then each side flash scenes
Of how the other side
Is being ignorant and mean

With prejudice they display
The pain and misery of their own
But leave the misery
Of the other side
Alone

For they need the populations
To finance and die in their wars
As they sit back in their fancy homes
And hire the poor to do their chores

They are the civil-lying men
Who pretend they are
More than what they really are

They hide behind
Each other's sin
And live large
In expensive homes
And drive fancy cars

The injuries of those who survive
Can sometimes be much harder to see
As they fight unseen battles hidden
As PTSD

For they are truly at war
Not only with each other
But they are at war with
Their inner selves

Shoot 'em up bang bang
It ain't no thang
Though it seems so strange
And somewhat deranged

That they fight and fight
To convince society
That what they are doing
And who they are screwing
Is somehow alright

They once were little boys
Who committed
Random acts of violence

But now they are part of
Massive armies that tandemly
In the name of civilization
Commit untold destruction
And death upon each other
In the name of their
Civilized nation

Convinced not to think
Of all human beings
As being their sister and brothers
With rage they engage
In destroying each other

They do not even care
What for
As long as they win
The War

"Civil War"

A civil war is being fought
It is a war to be civil
An existential threat
That is not trivial

It is spiritual in nature
Battles of character extremes
A house divided
Where democracy screams

Truth is not evident
As the pride of men
Unabashedly causes them
To act without repent

Internal battles are lost
By those too lazy to think

Led by their emotions
They follow crazies
With unnatural devotion
As morality sinks

A civil war fought
In an uncivilized nation
Where agreeing to hate
Makes strange relations

River of Truth

Relationships are based on
Political make pretends
As people turn their backs
On childhood friends

A civil war is being raged
Where civility disappears
And doing what is right
Gets lost in fear

It is a civil war
Where nobody wins
So let us stop the war
Before humanity ends

"Weapons of Instruction"

I wish that weapons had wings
When they fly into the sky
Perhaps they would go another place
Where people would not have to die

Bullets could dance above the rainbows
Like birds putting on a magnificent show
And show us how to work together
To navigate the currents of life
So that we can live and grow

And if bullets had their own mind
Maybe we could not force them
To be agents to destroy humankind
Then they could change direction
And find a safer way of correction

I wish that bombs were intelligent
More intelligent than man
Maybe they would find other ways
To solve the problems we do not understand

Bombs could explode in the air
And like fireworks that entertain
They could light up the sky
Rather than being used to cause us pain

River of Truth

Perhaps bombs and bullets will awaken
And show the world how to be kind
By going on a massive strike
And refuse to strike humankind

Maybe technology
Will not turn against us
If we program it for the good of all
For the things we think protect us
Can be used to make us fall

We have seen the damage of weapons
That beckons hearts of stone
But we are so obsessed with power
We find them hard to leave alone

We discriminate indiscriminately
As we harm and kill as if we are insane
Just like little boys playing with toys
But these toys cause death and pain

People look down on poor folks
As some destroy each other with zeal
While most of them pay taxes
To fight the rich man's wars
Where many more innocent are killed

Collateral damage they call it
As bombs and bullets fly everywhere
I wish that weapons could instruct us
To love each other when we are scared

Let us see the complete story
Not just the propagandized glory

Show the real price of war to humankind
The fatherless children left behind
The broken limbs the missing arms
The blinded eyes the families harmed

The ripple effects of children lost
Teach the truth about
What war really costs

The streaming tears the wasted years
Dark skies in the day as ashes fly
From trees and homes burned away

The uncivilized acts
And the abominations
Gone forever are daughters and sons
From every nation

Is this what we mean
When we define civilization

River of Truth

Show them what
Death and destruction really cost

Bombard them with knowledge
Then fill their hearts
With love never lost

With the speed of a bullet
And the power of a bomb
May weapons of destruction
Morph into words of instruction

Embalmed for all eternity
As a guide of how the power of might
Can be used for something
That is good and right

May the wisdom and insights
Of history and lessons learned
Morph this paranormal fantasy
Into a reality

In which the technology
Of destruction turns
Into an awesome godly fight
That saves us from
Annihilating ourselves
By using systems that unite

CHAPTER IV
TRUTH OR CONSEQUENCES

"It Is What It Is"

Do not worry about what was
And what is
Because it is what it is

And it was what it was
Locked in time forever
Never to be changed
Even if you try to
Rearrange it in your mind

So just be kind to yourself
Because it is what it is

The best help that you can get
Is to learn from the past
And stop having a fit
Over the things you cannot forget

Because it is what it is
And it ain't nothing
But real-life show biz

Your life is not a quiz to be answered
For you are the answer to your life
So be intentional about what you do
Because what you do is consequential

River of Truth

Stop being a big cry baby
And wondering about
All the maybes

Maybe if you did this
Maybe if you did that

Find some good in your choices
Then rejoice
Because it is what it is

Slow down
Relax
And release
Stop letting your emotions
Tax your peace

What you have done
Is a done deal

You cannot change the past
But at last
You can choose and change
How you feel

For once it is done
Whether you lost or won
Sad or mad
Found or hid

Whether the fault is
Hers or his
It is
What it is

"When the Skies Were Blue"

When the skies were blue
And hearts were pure
Man had enough
And wanted no more

The rain came
And satisfied thirst
Life was watered
Beneath the dirt

The earth was alive
And all life thrived
Symbiotically satisfied

All knew what to give
And take to survive

When the skies were blue
The beast roamed the land
Some died so others could live
But all returned to the earth

For their dust was meant to give
Nourishment for new birth
So the dead in life
Were rebirthed
As our relatives

It is just a circle
An endless loop
You cannot defeat it
No matter what you do

We cut down the trees
That clean the air we breathe
But man will fall
Before the forest submits

The more we rape the earth
The harder it will hit
Returning us to dirt
Defeated with our wit

And despite what we do

The heavens will return to
When the skies were blue
Even if we are not around
To enjoy the view

"Beautiful Sunsets"

Beautiful sunsets
Silhouetted in smog
As children sit
On crumbling doorsteps
Surrounded by man-made fog

Beautiful sunsets
Cast in truncated rainbows
But children cannot play
Because the air is too thick
With summer's dirty snow

Beautiful sunsets
Look so heavenly in the skies
But the air is so dense
Children cannot see
Through the flecks in their eyes

Beautiful sunsets
Cannot hide the smells
Deposited by greedy institutions
Whose leaders live far away
So their offspring
Have a haven
In which to play

Bright vibrant sunsets
Where there is no restitution
From the greed of the wealthy's
Atmospheric pollution

Beautiful sunsets
What a display

But I long for the times
Where all children can enjoy
Beautiful sunsets
Without moving far away

"In The State of California"

It causes cancer
In the state of California
But how about New Jersey
Where I am from

I do not see the same warning
In the Garden State
So
Do I have to run

It causes cancer
In the state of California
But how about the state of Delaware
Did they get the message too late

Because I did not see
Any warning
In the first state

It causes cancer
In the state of California
But how about other states like PA

If they ignore
California's warning
Will they be okay

It causes cancer
In the state of California
But is this just localized

Or are the people in California
Weaker than the other guys

And
If it causes cancer
In the state of California

Then why are they allowed
To sell their goods
In other neighborhoods

Is the government
Holding back
And not letting us know
The real facts

If it causes cancer
In the state of California
Then it causes cancer
Everywhere
Including all the USA

I thought I better warn ya
Because I want everyone to be okay

"Slave Meals"

We should riot
Over our slave meal diets
Though it does damage in ways
That we do not realize
Or immediately feel

So we flavor such waste
To appease our taste
And then we try it

As we survive
On our diet
Of slave meals

Hooked on grease crack
And fried food heart attacks
We unknowingly
Crave an early grave

Eating food based on
How we feel
Taste versus health

A paradigm conflicted
Where we become addicted
To our slave meals

Meals that the master
Used to throw away
Become the over-seasoned
Meals of today

Cooked in grease
In heavy griddles
And giving our arteries
A harmful crease

The taste of waste
Will chase you
Back and forth
To the hospital
Where you will fall apart
And be disabled

Therefore making you
The empty space
At the dinner table

But that will not stop us from
Putting chitterlings in our faces
Seasoned with hot sauce
Which were pork intestines with
Feces littering spaces
That should have been tossed

River of Truth

We even eat
Scavengers that craw
On the ocean floor
And feed on the dead

Supermarket pimps
Sell us crabs and shrimp
Then we salvage the taste
From said scavengers
That eat waste

We suck our fingers
To remove the juices
Of the dead
Sucking and sucking
Like we never been fed

But the real ringer is
I eat them too
Because I am just as hooked
As all of you

So come and join me
And feast
Suck your fingers
And smile

Then we can blame
Our bad health
And early deaths
On heredity

And continue to be in denial
That we could live longer
If we discontinued
Our slave meal life style

"Dead and Gone"

You do not have to boast
But you know
You miss me most

Now that I am
Dead and gone

You use to yawn
When I asked you
To spend some time
With only me

But now that I am
Dead and gone

You sing sad songs
Wishing
For my return

NOW you yearn
For the good old days
That you never took time
To enjoy with me

NOW you see the light

But it is too late
Much too late to
Make it right

Now
That I am
Dead
And gone

CHAPTER V
SWIMMING UPSTREAM

"Just A Thought"

As I looked at the sky
That holds back the space
That masks
The end of my mind

Where time no longer exists
And reality
Never changes
But just is
Exactly as it always was
In the great I Am

I became afraid
That this absolute truth
Would destroy
My I am-ness

So I eagerly returned
To find my individuality
In the sublimity
Of my ignorance

"Me Version of The King's English"

Him did this
Her did that

I know that him
Should be he
And that her
Should be she

But if you understand
Every word that I say
Then why question me
When I say it me way

It is a rapper's game that I play
The King's English
Is my choice to choose
Or disobey

Me create as me fantasize
Then take the words and
Create a surprise
As I synthesize
The improper English
That others despise

Me use linguistics
That make it realistic to me

Me so sorry you cannot see
Beyond formalities

Because you have been educated
In a way that forces you to stay
Trapped in a world
Where only your reflection can play

But me be liberated
Even if you correct the way me stated it
Me see beyond I when I say me
Even if you cannot appreciate
Me speaking creatively

Me original language was stolen
And that is the truth
So excuse me
If me does not sound
Exactly like you do

Correcting me
Might be your fetish
But you also screw up
The original King's British

And in your effort
To sound like you are in command
You use so many big words
That you are hard to understand

River of Truth

And the true purpose of
Communication
Is to create shared meaning
Not to be demeaning

So for now
My mister and misses
How I sound haters
And my uninvited educators

Me
See you later

"Mothers Man-boys and Deadbeat Dads"

Deadbeat dads who disappear
And leave their women to raise their sons
Have no idea
Of the potential damage that can be done

Women do the best they can
When dead-beat fathers
Neglect their responsibility
To raise their sons to be a man

As their deadbeat dads
Abandon them
Many man-boys grow up failing to understand
What it is to be a responsible man

Some women have allowed these man-boys
To rule their minds
Because they could not find
The strength to strap
What their bottom cast

So they have allowed them
To have the last word
When they frown
And get too hot to cool down

Sometimes these struggling mothers
Can be heard praying with a pulsating heart

River of Truth

Lord why am I failing life's course
By putting the horse before the cart

Some of these same women
Have allowed grown-up man-boy suitors
To abuse them to the point
That their bones get knocked out of joint

And some have lost their mental
Physical and spiritual health
To the point that they no longer
Believe in their selves
And lose faith in all men

These horrible man-boys
That have abused these women
Were the same man-boys
Who gave their mothers crap

But their mothers were too intellectual
When they gave them lip
To crack their hips
With a father thick strap

Then these man-boys
End up defining themselves
Through someone else's pain
Because they did not realize

And please get this
The deep pain they hide inside
Have caused them to capsize
Many of their relationships

They twist their cruelty
Into so many sorries
That you and I know they are not real
Because they are playing a game

But guilt from the past
Allow these man-boys
To steal their mother's joy
Just the same

And their deadbeat dads
Who left them and their mothers
All alone
Become a sorry a'... man-boy
In someone else's home

"Users Are Losers"

Users are losers
Confused and immature
They will keep using you
Until you say
No more

Users do not know their role
In you telling them no
Their goal is to control
All the seeds that you sow

They will sing symphonies
Of being needy
Knowing your sympathy
Hides how much they are greedy

Users will act like they are
Your best friend
As they take from you
As much as they can

They will never say no more
Unless you say stop
Because they live for
What other people got

What they do not take outright
They will try to borrow
And say they will pay you back
Someday
But never tomorrow

They will ask themselves over for lunch
Then try to borrow your clothes
Then sweet talk you
Until you forget what they owe

And when you ask them to pay you back
Without a doubt
They will act like they do not know
What you are talking about

When you get tired of them
They will get mad at you
For stop being the fool
That they can always use

But the more they take
The more they will lose
The opportunity to stand tall
In their own two shoes

But users are losers
Confused and immature
They will keep using you
Until you say

NO more

"Holler Happy Holidays"

No more Christmas with gift list
Programmed to get things soon missed
While Jesus is forgotten
In Xmas

Christ-mas gets pronounced as
Chris-mas
As bills pile up
While the celebration of God
Gets twisted

Then Easter funnies
Egg you on to believe
That bunnies drop eggs
Into candy-filled baskets
That prep teeth for future cavities

But not before
Children's conditioned behavior
To wish and ask for more
Comes with a failure to teach them
About the risen Savior
And what Easter really stands for

Then we celebrate
The Fourth of July
Without recognizing those
That have suffered and died from lies

River of Truth

Disguised as a patriotic cause
Just as fake as Santa Clause

Designed to protect assets
Of the wealthy and those in power
That brainwash us to think
Their cause is ours

Now let us not forget this
We take advantage of the dumbest
By celebrating
Christopher Columbus

A man whose heart
Was so callous
And filled with malice

He ordered the torturing
Of American natives
Who did not find enough gold
For the greedy Queen

Then tried to be creative
By calling them savages
When he was the one
Who was uncivilized and mean

Now some want us to step back
From all these facts

And have us afraid
To be woke

They rather have us
Intellectually broke
And stuck in their cults
Molded like clay
And looking for happiness
In all the wrong ways

Guided by an invisible collar
Of super marketing and sales
They make us want to holler
From all their tall tales

We leave a trail of money
Overspent
That we later repent
About how we spent
Our hard-earned pay

But all the while
With a great big smile
We still holler

Happy holidays

"A Stain In the Rain"

It was raining cows and horses
When I saw a Caucasian sister
Struggling in the rain

I just wanted to assist her
Without breaking any societal vows
Or cause others to complain

As the raindrops
Mopped the window panes
I cautiously approached her

But she looked so nervous
She barely turned around
Suddenly one of her bags dropped
To the dirty puddled ground

I wondered would she refuse
If I offered some friendly service
Or would her puzzled expression
Turn into a frown

But I said hi my sister
I just wanted to say hello
And have a nice day
Can I help you carry your groceries
Before the stormy weather
Blows them away

Or can I walk you in the rain
And cover you with my umbrella
Without you or the world
Being terrified of a white woman
Being befriended by a black fella

Just trying to be a good human

My only mission was to
Show her kindness and grace
For I am a Christian
And did not care
About the color of her face

But when she turned around
She seemed to be so afraid
That she could not
Look me directly in the eye

Still her trembling hands
Grasped the wet bags
That had fallen on the damp ground
Beneath the clouded sky

I found this to be stunning
And somewhat funny

For she'd rather get soaked in the rain
Than be caught by the perception

River of Truth

That a black man could be
Her object of affection

But without hesitation
I shamefully admit
I too was afraid
Of others' interpretation
And that they might have a fit

If they thought I was helping her
Just to see what I could get

But I thought
Forgive me my white sister
For failing to have the courage
To assist you and help you out

And not worry what I thought
What others thought about

For I chose not to come to her aid
Because I cared too much about
Society's racist shade

As I returned to my car
I turned around and saw

A smashed bottle of mustard
Mixed with wet leaves
Creating a strange potpourri
Of a memory of lost opportunity

As the accidental art washed away
Next to her abandoned shopping cart
It left a minute stain
On the cracked pavement

But an even bigger stain in my heart
Made me feel when we are too scared
To trust and show love for each other
It is a form of enslavement

Bound by emotional pain
It makes it harder to weather this
Thing called life
And our quest for happiness

Sometimes our doubt
Fear and pain
Is much harder to erase
Then a stain in the rain

CHAPTER VI

SPEAK LOVE

"Speak Love" (prologue)

Speak love
Speak love
Speak love
Speak love

Stop that attack
Speak love speak love
Pour into her
What you want coming back

Tell her that you love her
Every day
And show her that you love her
In every way

Speak love
Speak love
Speak love
Speak love

Provide and protect
Always love and serve
Speak to her with respect
And you will stroke love's nerve

With all your actions
Show her that you care

Speak soft sexy sounds
Into her sensitive ears

Speak love
Speak love
Speak love
Speak love

Do not speak to her terse
Do not fuss or complain
Never ever curse her
Speak words that ease her pain

Let your words reflect love
And a heart full of romance
Always edify her
With words of assurance

Speak love
Speak love
Speak love
Speak love

Use your voice
To give her a thrill
Because if you don't
Someone else will

Speak love

"Looking for A Good Knight"

I am looking for a good knight
To join me in the fight
To oppose evil
And do what is right

I am looking for a good knight
A keeper of the throne
A believer in the sanctity
Of making his home a happy home

A place guarded by
One who protects and puts smiles
On every face
Including his own

I am looking for a good knight
Void of vanity
And filled with an overflow
Of love and respect for his family

A love that comes from deep within
And a life so lived
That others will want to follow him

I am looking for a good knight
One who corrects himself
Without hesitation

River of Truth

So he can love and protect
His family and friends
And treat strangers
Like his relations

I am looking for a good knight
One who is willing to ride
A mule if need be
Instead of a thoroughbred horse

A man willing to make sacrifices
To keep his family's finances on course

A man who keeps his bills paid
Before he considers buying
An expensive Rolls Royce
Or a high-end Escalade

A good knight has a plan
And not just a dream
Because he is a man
That is much more than he seems

A man of nobility
With the ability to rise
Above the need to
Rise above all others

And the civility to be
Kind and not afraid to join me
In the brotherhood
Of those dedicated

Not just fighting for justice
In various strongholds
But exemplify it
In their household

A saintly man who follows
The example of Christ
Who chooses good over evil
And treats everyone nice

As they "good knight"
The darkness into day
Others will want to follow them
And not want to run away

I am looking for a good knight
A mature man of God
Ready for the crusade to
Fight against all that is not right

One who can overpower hades
With his inner light

River of Truth

The light of the Holy Spirit
He who stands against all evil
And never fears it

I am looking for a good knight
A man of honor
Who always gives his best

So that he can give his wife
His children
And the world
A good night's rest

"Boys And Men, A Lover's Anthem"

A teenage boy can screw you
But only a man can make love
Like he really knew you

Every spot you got
A man
Will turn winter
Into something hot

Every time
As he touches your heart
Not just your behind

Not to mention
He always pays attention
To your wants and needs
And puts them before his own

A man will feel so nice
Because his love
Is about self-sacrifice

His desire
Is to set you on fire
That is what boys do
After they are fully grown

River of Truth

He massages you all over
Without laying wood
Because his only intention
Is to make you feel good

He gets close to you
He likes your natural scent
Then barely touches you
Until you shake
Like you want to repent

He moves to your heartbeat
Faster and faster as you get excited
But knows when to slow down
Just like you like it

He pays attention
To how you breathe
He is the kind of lover
That will make you believe

He knows your entire body
Is a magnificent erogenous zone
And enjoys loving you
Until your screams become moans

He takes his time
He is never in a rush

This is how a man makes love
Beyond a boyhood crush

A man knows
That in the end
His detailed attention
Pays great dividends

"She Is A Woman (A Message To Our Men)"

She is more than you imagine
With a heart that is honest
And pure

She is a woman powerful
But your pride
Keeps you from seeing more

She cries in her laughter
But all you see is her smile
Stop acting like her master
She is a woman not a child

She has a voice much stronger
So much stronger than it seems
Her soprano is sweeter
Then the deepest bass
In your screams

Some do double the work you do
They have a job to help pay bills
Clean up after you and cook meals
Then love you until you are fulfilled

Mother sister aunt cousin friend
A woman is God's special gift to man
She will love you through thick and thin
Just know that she is a woman

"Love Yourself"

Love yourself
Because God has given you
All you need to be the best you
That you can be

Love yourself
Because you have
Every thing you need
Every thing for your personal wealth

Be not jealous of
What others have
What they look like
Or what they can do

Because the things
You were meant to have
Is more than enough for you

Your love for anyone else
Can only be true
When you love yourself too

We are so connected
With the perfection of
Every individual's uniqueness
A uniqueness forged by
Time and space

Giving fullness and
Beautiful color to this world
Emanating from every land
Culture and race

Love yourself
Because God's wonderful
Human mosaic
Cannot be complete
Without each human being
Including you and me

You are meant to be here
You are meant to be counted
You are meant to make a difference

You are meant to have peace
Prosperity and wealth
You are meant to have
The deepest love

If you believe we are created
In God's image
And you say you love God
And that God is love

Then you must love
All of humanity
Starting with loving yourself

"Long-stem Roses"

Hear that see that smell that
True that love is so sweet
Hear that see that smell that
Love just for me

I hold you to the sky
The rose of love I hold you high
You are like long-stem roses
Everyone knows this

You are sweeter than
An overdose of love

Never to be surpassed
We have an everlasting love
Blessed in the sky
From the heaven above

And I see your love notes
Written all over the clouds

And I am so proud
To see that you can be
That which I can love forever

My heart is stolen
On you I am holding
Holding all my love for you

River of Truth

You are smoother than
The riches wine
And finer than
I could ever imagine
For these eyes to see

You and I
We make the flower
Stem and rose
In love devoured

On solid ground
I plant my stem
So long to reach
Your love within

Soaking wet
You rain on me
And I am more
Than I could ever see

The flower held
We make complete
So pretty on
Our love-soaked sheet

My stem
I save
Just for you

You are so beautiful
Just like long-stem roses
Everyone knows this

Hear that see that smell that
True that love is so sweet
Hear that see that smell that
Love just for me

Just like long-stem roses
Everyone knows this
You are sweeter than
An overdose of love

"Speak Love" (epilogue)

1 Corinthians 13; 4-8, New International Version

Speak love
Speak love
Speak love
Speak love

Love is patient
Love is kind
It does not envy
It does not boast
It is not proud

Speak love
Speak love
Speak love
Speak love

It does not dishonor others
It is not self-seeking
It is not easily angered
It keeps no record of wrongs

Speak love
Speak love
Speak love
Speak love

Love does not delight in evil
But rejoices with the truth

It always protects
Always trusts
Always hopes
Always preserves

Love never fails

Speak love
Speak love
Speak love
Speak love

CHAPTER VII
THE RIVER SPEAKS

"I Still See You"

I saw you
In the beginning
And I will
Still see you in the end

You cannot hide from Me
I am omnipresent
The Great I Am
The God that you cannot see

You do not talk to Me
Like you used to
And you still eat
From the forbidden tree

But there is no shade
Where you can hide
From Me
Because I still see you

I gave you freedom of choice
Free to select death or life
You want the riches
But not the sacrifice

River of Truth

You want
The convenience
Without
The obedience

I have heard everything you pray
But until you line up with My word
You will ruin the home
I have given you to stay

Though I gave you enough
For all your needs
You destroy your gifts
To satisfy your greed

I may seem to you
To disappear in your pride
As you deny Me with
Your actions and words

But the thought that
From Me you can hide
Is an abomination
That is so absurd
Because

I
Still
See
You

"Men of God"

Fighting killing
Willing to call His name
In vain

They cry
As they light up the sky
With tracers of light
That flash in the night
As men women and
Children die

Some lie unattended on
Blood-soaked grounds
In unimaginable pain

With burnt skin bullet holes
Man's sin becomes
A baseless claim of victory
With false gains

Documented as
Collateral damage
Their rockets fly
To give them an advantage

They ask for mercy
When they are to blame

River of Truth

For most of the misery
Because they are the enemy
Even if they rewrite history

Men of God
Call on their deities
To empower them
To kill more

So they can declare victory
Without appearing
To neglect moral responsibility
For their endless
Uncivilized wars

Men of God
Choose their clan as brothers
As they separate into
Them those and the others

How flighty they can be
As they cause suffering
While declaring
To know The Almighty

They separate into
Denominations sects and
Various religions

And take God's word
Out of context
As they make their
Evil decisions

They ask for blessings
From the great Him
While confessing
Their intentional sins

Some of these religious men
Treat minorities and women
Like second-class citizens

Then go to mosque temples
Churches and synagogues
And act like
Only they serve God

They declare themselves
To be right
While their created enemies
Are wrong

But how can they worship God
By saying others do not belong

They call Him the great I Am
Allah Buddha and Yahweh

But it does not matter
What name they say
When they deny God
With their selfish ways

Men of God
Claim to be masters on earth
But cannot master
Their own self worth

So they hide in their pride
As they falsify being
Sanctified

Singing hallelujah
They steal land
Ravish and rape women
Brainwash children and adults
And make their demands

While they declare
They are under
God's command

Some go to church on Friday
When the sun goes down
Then wage war
To gain more ground

Others sing
Sunday hallelujahs
That fails to turn away
The heated hate
Practiced every day

As they hide the truth
On the fourth of July
Men glorify war
More than God is glorified

And their belief goes
Where their faith never trods
All this they do
In the name of God

Then men of God distort the facts
As they find passages in the bible
To try to justify their sinful acts

But in the end
Their soul is sold
To gain the riches
Of fool's gold

Men of God
Walk tall in pride
So high they cannot see
The sin they try to hide

River of Truth

They know religion
But if they really knew God
They would make
Much different decisions

Because men of God
When you are mean
The end does not justify
The means

Nor does saying you are sorry
Without changing your ways
Make you clean

Believe repent submit
Commit to the risen Christ

Only then will you know
How to show the world
That you are willing
To pay the price
To be true men of God

"Denominations the Religion Division"

Sometimes
Religious denominations
Can be an abomination

A false story of God's word
Being taken from
What is heard out of context
By those too lazy to read
What comes before or next

They do not study the bible
For its truth is liable to make them change
Instead they accept the words of others
Even when they sound very strange

They lock onto a few verses
And form denominations
Reinforced with rituals that claim
That is the only way to salvation

And in all this malarky
They walk with pride
As they form hierarchies
Where their sins can easily hide

And some of these same people
Live their lives like God is not real

River of Truth

As they distort the truth
Based on what they feel

They create a grey area
That allows them to do their worst
Choosing what is best for them
They distort God's word
As they hide behind their hurt

While others try to hide
By running
From church to church

They divide themselves into
Micro religious nations
And preach the only road to heaven
Is through their denomination

They give themselves an assignment
That is out of alignment
With the word and will of God

Thus the bible becomes liable
To many interpretations
Meticulously enforced by
Ultra-religious squads

So people do their own thing
Claiming freedom through denominations
That reinforce beliefs that have little to do
With the contextual biblical truth revelations

Then they sleep
Because they are afraid
If they are awakened by the truth

God will not forgive them
Because they know
Just what they do

"Stop In the Name of God"

Freeze frame
All your pain
And stop
In the name of God

Think and pray
Before you complain
Guard your mouth
From all disdain

Stop
In the name of God

Examine the ways
You use your free will
Is your soul worth
All the thrills

The lies
Bad relationships
Drugs and pills

The gossip exchanged
And all your blaming
And the negative thoughts
You are sustaining

Stop
In the name of God

Meditate on things
That are good and pure
Stop stepping over yourself
And always wanting more

Use your divine discernment
To help you see things done and said
The physical mental and spiritual places
Where you should not tread

You cannot be tempted
Beyond that which you can bear
Activate your faith
And start your prayer

It is not too late
To avoid disaster
Give it all
To the Almighty Master

Stop
In the name of God

Study your bible
And daily devotions
Let God guide you through
All your pain and emotions

Stop acting like
You are
The only one that suffers

Stop
In the name of God

Be silent
Be still
And
Let Thy will be done

Stop your sin
And meditate
On Him

Stop
In the name of God

"Sin No More"

Today's sin
Today's pleasure
Tomorrow's pain
And lost treasure

A prison is created
By decisions made
As the truth gets clouded
By our charade

Weeping and wailing
And prayers denied
There is no repentance
Within ceaseless cries

No change of ways
Is the cause
When there is no commitment
To God's laws

When men follow the path
Of man's ways
And have no fear of God's wrath
And live for today

River of Truth

So many mistakes
Will be repeated
They will lose sight
Of when they are defeated

So time
And time again
They will suffer
As they are lost

Not realizing
Their senseless sin
Always
Must pay a cost

Even when men
Sin with shame and regret
Their life is still wasted
If they forget

Just saying you are sorry
Is not enough
Because without a change of ways
It is just a bluff

But many will be tormented
By truth denied
And suffer more
When they realize

The true meaning
Of repentance
And what happens
When their joy
Meets sin's
Many consequences

"Return to Thee"

We are made nought
But of the dust
Under the sod
Of the earth

Animated
To give birth to
The love and glory
Of God

We whisper
In each other's ears
As if we
Are on trial

And false greatness
Disappears
Into the darkness
Of our denials

This greatness
Baked only
In the oven
Of our brain

Gives birth to the disdain

Of our honesty to admit
We are lost
And no longer walk with God

So it remains
As the world crumbles
Under the footprint
Of our blindness

We stumble
But still we discreetly
Walk tall

For we are afraid
To look down
And recognize
Our kindred
To the dirt
Beneath our feet

When we are silent
We hear truth
Pulling us towards
The light

But we become too
Preoccupied with ourselves
To follow the path
Of righteousness

River of Truth

Thus we blame God
And the world
For our blight
And where we are at

Because we
Do not realize
Most of us
Made it like that

So in our darkness
We are lost
Only to become
Pieced together

By the bad choices
That we make
As we fail
To take notice
 Of the life
That we create

Looking for easy outs
And pacifiers
We go through life
Gathering things
Things that do not make sense

Then we surround ourselves
With liars
That give the false pretense
That all is well

But it is a path
That leads to hell
A selfish life
Of greed and lust

Where our only salvation
Is to choose God
Before we return
To the earthly dust

"I Call Your Name"

I call Your name
In deep prayer
I call Your name

In a world
That has lost its way
To Thee
Only to You I pray

I pray that we are strengthened
With moral ethical
And Godly assurance
And live
With love's
Protective endurance

I pray humanity
Will live and give
Like all of us
Are inseparable relatives

I call Your name

I pray that hate dissipates
And people realize
Their quest
For worldly domination

Separates them from
The gift of Your salvation

I call Your name

I pray that parents
Parent their children
As parents
Not friends
And hold them
To higher values
Beyond make pretend

I pray that the youth
Respect their parents and elders
And are given direction
And examples
That show love
Forgiveness
And affection

I call Your name

Sometimes I pray at home
In every room far and near
And call Your name
To fill the atmosphere

River of Truth

Other times
I walk or ride
And pray for the strangers
That pass me by

Then I call Your name
To bless them who suffer
With
And without blame

I say amen
To my word
I know my voice
In You is heard

Sometimes I lose control
Forgive me Lord
With dry eyes I cry deep
Within my soul

I pray for my soul
I pray
For my self-control

Help me to obey
And be mindful
Of what I do and say

For only in Thee
Do I trust
For the world's sin
You came

So I call Your name

My soul calls out
Only to You
Jesus Christ

My River of
Love and Truth

ABOUT THE AUTHOR

Mr. Isaac Brown Jr. was born and raised in the small town of Salem, New Jersey, and has lived in New Castle, Delaware, for over 40 years. He graduated *magna cum laude* with a degree in Psychology from Widener University in Chester, Pennsylvania. He is excited to present his second book of original poems, which reflects his insights and emotional responses to both past and present life experiences.

Mr. Brown began writing poetry at the age of 11. In addition to poetry, he has authored plays and co-written several songs.

One of his recent lyrical achievements includes writing the words to the song "Hurry Up Tomorrow", featuring music composed by his cousin, Daryl Howard, and performed by the Nurons, which was sampled by three-time Grammy Award winner *The Weeknd*! The track appears on The Weeknd's album *Hurry Up Tomorrow*.

Isaac is also the author of *I See You, A Poetic Experience* and contributed a chapter to the book *Let Us Make a*

Man. His work has been featured in Newark Delaware's ongoing literary project, *Dreamstreets* magazine. His poem "I Am That I Am," originally selected for *Dreamstreets*, is also included in his book *River Of Truth*.

www.ingramcontent.com/pod-product-compliance
Lightning Source LLC
Chambersburg PA
CBHW071242070526
44583CB00017B/2299